THE PERSONALITY OF LEADERSHIP

HOW TO SELECT AND DEVELOP GREAT LEADERS

BY

JAMES C. VELGHE

ISBN-10: 1481961268
EAN-13: 9781481961264

This book is available at:

CreateSpace www.createspace.com/4128826

Amazon www.amazon.com/dp/1481961268

Ingram http://www.ingramcontent.com/Pages/Retailers.aspx

Other retail outlets

Contents

V. DESIRED LEADERSHIP CHARACTERISTICS . 113

Acknowledgments

I wish to thank all of my clients over the years for contributing to the research that made this book possible. It was only with their trust and confidence that we were able to provide the leadership assessment, measure the performance of their leaders, and survey the opinions and work values of their employees.

To all of the consultants and staff of my old firm, Management Science Associates, Inc. (MSA), and my current firm, Work Dynamics, Inc., I convey my respect, admiration, and gratitude. Without their hard work, loyalty, and dedication, none of this work would have been possible. I also would like to express my gratitude to my friend and colleague, Rita Tripp, RN, MBA, JD, who has worked with the leadership assessment for more than twenty-five years and assisted me in writing this book. A special note of thanks goes to Ed Hume, who, along with his colleagues at Hume,

Mansfield, and Silber, developed the original leadership assessment.

Finally I want to thank Dr. Vincent Flowers and Debra Heflich, who graciously helped me at a critical time to refocus and refine my knowledge of work value analysis. It was their intimate knowledge and application of Graves's levels of psychological existence theory—combined with Dr. Flowers's tireless passion for truth and knowledge—that inspired me to continue my own work. Their knowledge of Dr. Graves's theory, levels of psychological existence, and work value analysis is beyond measure.

Introduction

Looking back over the long history of our management consulting experience, we have been blessed to have worked with some of the most successful and complex corporations in the United States. At one point we were retained by more than one thousand of these corporations, most of which were in the healthcare industry. With all of this experience, we have learned that no decision is more critical than leadership selection, and the higher the position of responsibility, the more critical the decision.

From our work in these corporations, we learned a great deal about senior leadership, through our own personal interactions and through the consulting tools and methodologies we used to diagnose management issues and assess leadership effectiveness. The following three consulting methodologies proved to be the most reliable and effective tools to evaluate leadership talent, enhance leadership effectiveness, and measure leadership success.

Leadership Assessment

In the mid-1970s, we first began to use a specialized personality assessment tool based on the trait theory of leadership to identify potential leaders and develop existing leaders. We used this assessment tool in hundreds of client organizations to select and develop thousands of leaders. Over the course of time, this assessment has proven consistently accurate and reliable. It has been extensively field-tested to say the least.

Work Value Analysis

Early in our consulting practice we developed an employee opinion survey to measure both job satisfaction and work values. More than 1.5 million employees were surveyed, and more than 800,000 work values were measured. Unlike the leadership assessment, which measures personality characteristics and traits, the work value analysis measures levels of psychological existence, and from this what a person values in work. Work value analysis has proven to be an invaluable tool in enabling leaders to meet the psychological work-related needs of their employees and helping them reach their full leadership potential.

Leadership Performance Measurement

If you want to measure a leader's success you must measure his or her actual job performance. Over the years, in our consulting practice, having observed the ineffective use of subjective performance measures, we developed and refined a quantifiable results-oriented methodology to measure leadership performance. We installed this methodology in hundreds of corporations for use by governing boards and CEOs as a means to objectively determine appropriate annual salary increases and bonus incentives based upon both corporate and individual executive performance. Although the methodology was the same for each client corporation, the application was unique to each client based on internal and industry benchmarks. Measurable objectives were set each fiscal year with acceptable ranges of performance, and at the end of the year, each executive was evaluated based upon his or her performance results. We learned a great deal about how an individual's personality characteristics and work value influence his or her ability to lead others and achieve results.

What to Expect

Whether you're a seasoned CEO, experienced corporate executive, aspiring leader, or budding entrepreneur, you will find the information in this book valuable and insightful. It is deliberately short on theory and long on practicality.

After reading this book you should have a sharper eye to size up potential leaders as well as a keener sense of what's behind the leadership behavior of both yourself and others. Hopefully you will be able to understand, relate to, and engage your colleagues and employees with greater insight, clarity, and precision.

Chapter I

About Leadership

Leadership has been described as "a process of social influence in which one person can enlist the aid and support of others in the accomplishment of a common task."[1] Other definitions of leadership from noted authorities include: "The only definition of a leader is someone who has followers" (Peter Drucker); "Leadership is influence—nothing more, nothing less" (John C. Maxwell); and "Leadership is a function of knowing yourself, having a vision that is well communicated, building trust among colleagues, and taking effective action to realize your own leadership potential" (Warren Bennis).

People define leadership in many different ways. Perhaps this is why in hundreds of our firm's leadership

---

[1] Chemers, M. 1997. *An Integrative Theory of Leadership*. New York: Psychology Press.

workshops so many participants have given such diverse definitions for the concept. Given the many theories, styles, and traits of leadership offered by various scholars, authors, and consultants over the years, it is not surprising that there is a bit of confusion regarding the definition of leadership and what to look for when attempting to hire an outstanding leader. Let's begin with leadership theory.

Over the years many theories of leadership have emerged. Some of the most noted include trait theories, behavioral and style theories, situational and contingency theories, functional theory, integrated psychological theory, transactional and transformational theories, leader-member exchange theory, and neo-emergent theory. Our work is based on both the trait leadership theory and the integrated psychological leadership theory. In our opinion the combination of these two leadership theories combines the best of all theories by not only recognizing, identifying, and using personality characteristics and traits to help select effective leaders, but also by enabling leaders to develop and enhance their leadership skills and abilities and adapt their leadership style and approach to the level of psychological existence and disparate work values of those they lead.

Without question the trait theory has proven over time to be a viable approach to the study and selection of leaders.[2] In simple terms, the trait theory states that individual traits influence leaders' abilities, and these traits accompany the individual from one leadership position to the next.[3] Most trait theories argue that great leaders are born, not made. Current studies, however, indicate that leadership is much more complex and cannot be boiled down to just a few key individual traits. Any one trait or set of traits does not necessarily make an extraordinary leader. Leadership traits of an individual—such as intelligence, assertiveness, or physical attractiveness, for example—do not change

---

[2] Kenny, D. A. and Zaccaro, S. J. 1983. "An Estimate of Variance Due to Traits in Leadership." *Journal of Applied Psychology* **68**: 678-685.

[3] Lord, R. G. et al. A Meta-Analysis of the Relation Between Personality Traits and Leader Perceptions: An Application of Validity Generalization Procedures. *Journal of Applied Psychology* 71: 402-410.

from situation to situation; rather each key trait may be applied to situations differently, depending on the circumstances. In our own experience, a person's work value influences the leadership application of his or her personality characteristics and traits.

Jon P. Howell, business professor at New Mexico State University, authored an insightful book titled *Snapshots of Great Leadership.*[4] In this book he describes the characteristics of **determination and drive**, which include traits such as initiative, energy, assertiveness, perseverance, and sometimes dominance as factors that influence leaders to actively pursue their goals, work long hours, demonstrate ambition and be competitive. Leaders with **cognitive capacity**—which includes intelligence, analytical skills, verbal ability, flexibility, and good judgment—are able to formulate solutions to difficult problems, work well under stress or deadlines, adapt to changing situations, and create well-thought-out plans. **Self-confidence**—which encompasses the traits of high self-

---

[4] Howell, J. P. 2012. *Snapshots of Great Leadership.* New York: Routledge.

esteem, assertiveness, emotional stability, and self-assurance—tends to reduce self-doubt and enhance a leader's ability to make decisions. Leaders with **integrity**—demonstrated by their being truthful, trustworthy, principled, consistent, dependable, and loyal—tend to impart these values to their followers. The trait of **sociability**—which describes individuals who are friendly, extroverted, tactful, flexible, and interpersonally competent—helps enable leaders to be accepted and to use diplomatic or collaborative measures to resolve issues.

Some critics of trait leadership theory ask, "If particular traits are key features of leadership, how do we explain people who possess those qualities but are not leaders?" Our answer to that question is simple. These individuals probably should be leaders but haven't been identified, haven't received the opportunity, or simply do not want to take on the role and responsibility of leadership. We see this often in healthcare, where some physicians and nurses possess all the desired characteristics and traits of leadership but do not want to give up treating patients and being a healthcare provider. They often say, "My calling is to be a caregiver—not a manager." There also are informal leaders who do not possess a formal leadership title but whose natural leadership characteristics and traits rise to the surface and enable them to informally have followers.

The integrated psychological theory of leadership began to attract more attention after the publication of James Scouller's *The Three Levels of Leadership* (2011).[5] Scouller argues that the older theories offer only limited assistance in developing a person's ability to lead effectively. He points out, for example, the following:

- Trait theories, which tend to reinforce the idea that leaders are born—not made— might help us select leaders, but they are less useful for developing leaders.

- An ideal style (e.g., Blake and Mouton's team style) does not suit all circumstances.

---

[5] Scouller, J. 2011. *The Three Levels of Leadership: How to Develop Your Leadership Presence, Knowhow and Skill.* Cirencester, UK: Management Books 2000.

- Most situational/contingency and functional theories assume that leaders can change their behavior to meet differing circumstances or widen their behavioral range at will, when in practice many find it hard to do so because of unconscious beliefs, fears, or ingrained habits. Thus leaders must work on their inner psychology.

- None of the old theories successfully addresses the challenge of developing leadership presence—that certain "something" in leaders that commands attention, inspires people, wins their trust, and makes followers want to work with them.

In our experience the integrated psychological theory of leadership combines the key strengths of trait theory, behavioral/style theory, situational theory, and functional theory by emphasizing the need for leaders to self-develop beyond their inherited personality characteristics and traits. Such self-development includes but is not limited to interpersonal skills, communication skills, motivational skills, and mastery of work values and levels of psychological existence. Such self-development enables leaders to adapt their leadership style and approach to the disparate work values of those they are leading, which results in a leadership that not only achieves corporate results but also meets the psychological work value needs of employees. This approach also provides a platform for leaders who may want to apply the philosophies of servant leadership which is an emerging management philosophy today, especially in nonprofit organizations.[6]

[6] Spears, L. C. Regent University. 2005. The Understanding and Practice of Servant-Leadership. https://www.regent.edu/acad/global/publications/sl_proceedings/2005/spears_practice.pdf.

Chapter II

Personality Characteristics
That Affect Leadership

M ore than six billion of us live on this planet, yet no two of us are alike. Our differences reflect not only our physical DNA but also our distinctive actions and our unique personal appearances. Our actions reveal our character traits, which in turn reveal our personality. Our unique blend of personality characteristics, levels of psychological existence, and the emphasis we place on them is what makes us unique. This makes us who we are—one in six billion. "Personality is defined as a unique blend of traits characterizing individuals and influencing their interaction with their environment".[7] The terms "personality,"

---

[7] Jackson, D. N. 1973. "Structured Personality Assessment." *Handbook of General Psychology*, ed. Benjamin B. Wolman (Englewood Cliffs, NJ: Prentice-Hall, 1973)..

"characteristics," and "traits" are used interchangeably throughout this book.

Our firm has applied the trait theory of leadership in measuring key personality characteristics and traits in thousands of leaders in hundreds of corporations. Over time these key characteristics and traits have proven consistently to be accurate predictors of effective and successful leaders. Whereas each of these individual characteristics and traits on the surface appears to be straightforward, it is important to emphasize that each cannot be viewed in isolation; rather they must be viewed in combination with one another. Even though there are only seven musical notes, it's the combinations of these seven musical notes that give rise to more melodies than one ever can hear. Even though there are no more than three primary colors, the combination of these colors produces more subtle hues than one ever can see. So is the case of these leadership personality characteristics and traits. It's the combination that tells the story and gives the true picture of the leader. In the following pages, we describe each of these characteristics and traits and provide some insight as to what they mean. As much as we would like, it is impossible for us to describe every combination and nuance that typically would be present in an individual assessment. From the following descriptions, however, you will gain insight into ten key personality characteristics and their effects on leadership behavior.

Dominance

The behavior to which this label refers is also known as assertiveness, boldness, aggressiveness, or social ascendancy. People who are not very forceful are considered timid, socially backward, shy, bashful, or retiring. For a leadership position that requires constantly meeting people and making a positive impression, there is an advantage in hiring someone who is socially dominant. People who are not particularly forceful are not at a disadvantage when they are dealing with people they know well—only people whom they have met for the first time or those they do not know well. Some people may be quiet or shy because they have not learned how to assert themselves. This is a trait that tends to change and can improve with the experience of public speaking or the deliberate choice to self-develop and work on extensive social contact, communication, and interpersonal skills. We typically look at the dominance and confidence factors together. A high dominance level or a lower confidence level may indicate a problem. For example an extremely high dominance score may indicate some hostility and a need to be domineering. While a mid-level leadership position may not require high dominance and confidence, we have found it to be a strategic advantage for chief executive officers and other senior leadership positions to score higher on this factor. The higher these scores, the more leadership "presence" the individual will have.

Self-Confidence

Self-confidence can be described as an absence of self-concern or self-consciousness in social situations. It means being at ease socially or being relaxed and uninhibited in the presence of others. Poised individuals may be aware of their effect on others, but knowing this does not hinder them or make them feel inhibited. People who are concerned about how others react to them, whether they have social acceptance, or whether others like them typically score low on this measure. The word "confidence" in everyday use can have a somewhat different meaning from what is intended here and usually refers to confidence in one's abilities. That may be a component of this measure, but the primary emphasis is upon social confidence. Again we typically look for an average to above-average score on this factor. The higher the leadership position, the greater our desire to see a higher score.

Individuals who have a high degree of social confidence are comfortable in their own skin. People who lack social confidence may engage others and be comfortable on a one-on-one basis, but if you put them in a room with a large group of people, they are suddenly filled with anxiety.

People who have a great deal of social confidence are far more likely to reach out to their employees, making themselves visible throughout the organization, as compared to leaders who stay in the executive suite and rarely get out among employees because they lack social confidence. With effort, the social confidence of leaders can and often does change over the course of their careers, especially if they make it a priority.

The Combination of Dominance and Self-Confidence

Confidence and dominance are two characteristics that must be viewed together. Both refer mostly to one's social interactions. The nice thing about dominance and confidence is these characteristics are usually fairly apparent if you spend a few hours with the candidate.

Today many boards expect their CEOs to establish and build relationships with all stakeholders of the corporation: investors, community leaders, and employees, and, in hospitals, the medical staff. There is therefore a real advantage to hiring a CEO who is comfortable meeting and establishing him or herself with new groups of people. If you want a leader with a presence, hire someone who scores high in both dominance and confidence. If executive presence is not a high priority, there is less need to be concerned with the candidate's dominance and confidence. That said, people who score below average on the dominance factor will be reticent to verbalize their opinions and may need to be "drawn out" in order for you to persuade them to engage and speak up in meetings.

Independence

Here we measure an individual's degree of sociability. People who score high in this area are socially independent; those who score low are dependent on others. Interaction is an important aspect of self-sufficiency. The highly sociable person who is everyone's friend is likely to score low on this measure. He or she finds it difficult to be critical of people, to act without the approval of others, or to deny custom or tradition. When situations are unclear, lines of authority are lacking, no precedents are established, or the problems are new, dependent people are more likely to appeal to those around or above them for support or direction. Dependent people may do this even when they may have solutions in their own minds. They have learned to trust others rather than their own judgment.

At times highly independent people may appear low in independence because they have withdrawn from interaction, and while they are coping with the demands of the situation, they are going through the motions. Truly dependent people, on the other hand, will give full cooperation. Highly independent people often refuse to interact because doing so threatens their strong need for autonomy. They need to assume sole responsibility for what they do and are most often those who complain about not having enough authority. For these individuals responsibility comes from within. It is dependent people who ask for responsibility from others.

Highly independent people are likely to resent being told how to do things. By contrast, dependent people

are cooperative, team players, and sharers of responsibility. They usually will welcome knowing not only what
is expected but also whether the methods or ideas are
acceptable to others. These people can seemingly grow
in independence on the job. This is because, in learn-
ing the job, they learn the rules or policies by which
they are governed. This imposed structure is not a burden; in their minds it gives them freedom to act. It is
ambiguous situations that block socially dependent
people. "Self-determined," "aloof," "indifferent to social
considerations," and "stubborn" are all terms applied to
independent people. These people are also highly selec-
tive in what they choose to do. As a result they structure
their own social environments.

In our experience, leaders in the middle range are
best able to interact or be interdependent with their
bosses, colleagues, and staff. Leaders with a great deal
of dependency are too much in need of others to interact effectively and may not always be objective enough
in their dealings with others. Leaders who are strongly

independent may simply refuse to interact with colleagues, bosses, or staff.

The people who score low on independence are the people at the water cooler. They have such a strong need for social interaction that they find it impossible to work alone; when checking references you probably will find they are very well liked. Conversely, highly independent people are out there "doing their own thing." They prefer to be left alone to do their jobs. When we were hiring high-performance, talented consultants for many years, we recognized that the job required them to travel alone, and even though they had full support from their managers, the office staff, and me, they were called upon to function very independently. So we made sure we only hired those who were independent, because, except for the time they were on site and engaged with a client, they truly functioned alone. Highly independent people love that. On the other hand, managing a group of highly independent consultants can be a little like herding cats. Anyone who ever has been responsible for managing a large group of physicians knows gaining consensus can be very difficult, as most physicians are not only smart but also gifted, talented, and very independent. These attributes, coupled with their high level of persistence, are why they made it through the rigors of medical school and their residencies. As one who has been responsible for leading highly independent people, I will tell you that I enjoyed every minute of it.

Initiative

Initiative is a variable concerned with attitudes and behavior that are preparatory to—or concurrent with—commitment and decisiveness. This definition also implies the ability to establish values or priorities independently. Initiative is the taking of responsibility.

Leaders who score high on this measure do their own thinking and planning and have little need to consult with others before they act. Low-scoring leaders usually need approval or direction before they feel comfortable taking action. In essence low scorers work on the basis of team effort, what others think, existing policies, or the direction of their bosses.

Decisiveness should be clearly differentiated from impulsiveness. People with much initiative or decisiveness are not always the first to act or commit, as is the case with impulsive individuals. They can tolerate uncertainty or ambiguity quite well.

Another correlate of highly initiative people is their possible rejection or indifference to externally imposed direction. Unless their independence is tempered by a responsiveness to the power of others (e.g., being politically astute), they are likely to act quite autonomously. This may not be acceptable in a strongly team-oriented organization, as these individuals are much more likely to want to work out things on their own rather than execute someone else's plan. They will be confident, however, of their own abilities in doubtful situations.

Initiative is not a matter of giving someone a set of facts and asking for a decision. People with initiative decide for themselves which facts are important and, on that basis, make their decisions. These leaders are much more likely to feel handicapped by limitations placed on their power or autonomy. They do not need responsibility, because for them responsibility is always present. It is merely a matter of choosing to do what is most important, as they see it.

In our experience most CEOs hope to hire leaders with high initiative who will keep them informed, but who will function independently, make decisions and carry out their responsibilities. There are of course some exceptions, such as someone who has micro-management control issues, wants to make all the decisions, and doesn't trust their subordinate leaders to make good decisions on their own. In these instances, hiring a highly independent person with high initiative and a great deal of confidence in his or her own decision-making will lead to frustration all around. In the long run, it can be a disservice to an organization to hire leaders who have low initiative and need a great deal of direction to run their operations. Those people are better suited in roles where they receive direction regarding how to do their jobs or have clearly defined policies and procedures that outline their jobs. Leadership we believe is a role that should encourage the exercise of initiative and independent judgment.

Most corporations have clearly thought-out policies and procedures that outline how a job should be done and the rules that must be followed. As a result, individuals with only average or below-average initiative and corresponding levels of confidence in their own decision-making can survive and sometimes even thrive in their leadership roles, depending on the support system around them and the strength of their other personality characteristics. That is not to say, however, that it is ideal. They will still need affirmation of their decisions and more than likely will take longer to make decisions than their counterparts who have higher initiative and corresponding high levels of confidence in their own decision-making.

Conversely, individuals who score off the chart on independence, initiative, and persistence may be better suited as entrepreneurs rather than work for a micromanager or for an organization that is very process oriented. They may get frustrated with the bureaucracy, while others may perceive them as not being able to "play well in the sandbox."

One interviewing technique to determine whether candidates have high initiative and subsequent confidence in their own decision-making is to say, "Tell me your story." If they have high initiative and a great deal of confidence in their decision-making, they typically, without hesitation, will begin to tell you their story. They will not ask you where you want them to start, because they have confidence that they know how to best tell their own story. They don't need your direction. On the other hand, people who lack initiative and confidence in their decision-making will respond to your query by asking, "Where do you want me to start?" They lack the confidence to decide for themselves where to start with their own story. If they say, "Do you want me to start from the beginning?" it indicates that they need your affirmation, and should you offer them a job, they will need affirmation from others before they make decisions.

Persistence

Persistence is the ability to persevere in the face of implied, anticipated, or actual social resistance. In the pursuit of their goals, people with a high persistence score may be viewed as thick skinned, stubborn, or indifferent to others. The goals or objectives need not be of their own choosing, as they may be executing the plans or ideas of others.

Leaders with low scores express concern for how others may think about them to the point that it may prevent them from getting things done. In this case they may need support or encouragement from their bosses or others in authority in order to endure. They also express a concern for others, which is often genuine, and therefore, they are typically sensitive rather than blunt.

We should note that one particular form of persistence or perseverance is only partially measured by this variable. Many people can be persistent or show a lot of follow-through, providing it does not involve interacting with people. The persistent measurement covers essentially tough-minded, socially interactive leadership behavior.

A large component of persistence is directness. Leaders with a high score typically are not evasive and are realistic. They deal forthrightly with situations, people, or their own feelings. In achieving their goals, they are often more intent upon what they are doing and what they want to get done rather than how others may perceive or react to them. Thus they can work on something for a long time without encouragement or prodding from others. They do not feel uncomfortable being different or unconventional. Individuals who score high on persistence at times may appear to be indifferent to others; in reality they are just highly focused on their work.

In our experience, persistence is the best predictor of success. That is because people who are very persevering do not give up until they reach their goals. Stories abound of highly successful individuals who overcame huge obstacles to achieve notoriety in some area.

Another way of thinking about the highly persevering person is the steady Eddie who keeps his head down and gets the job done. These are the people who don't need anyone to pat them on the back for work well done. They were reared in homes where they were taught never to give up. If you tell these people they can't do something, it just makes them try harder.

When it comes to persistence, this poem by Calvin Coolidge says it all.

Persistence

Nothing in the world can take the place of Persistence.

Talent will not;

Nothing is more common than unsuccessful men with talent.

Genius will not;

Unrewarded genius is almost a proverb.

Education will not;

The world is full of educated derelicts.

Persistence and determination alone are omnipotent.

The slogan 'Press on' has solved

And always will solve the problems of the human race.

Flexibility

In measuring flexibility we are gauging the individual's ability to change, to compromise, and to adapt to changing situations. Leaders who are high in flexibility find it easy to compromise, modify their goals, and/or adjust their tactics and methods according to the conditions. Leaders who score low in flexibility, however, are much more rigid in their thinking, particularly in situations and positions of high stress.

It is easy for individuals who score low on this factor to see weaknesses in others while also fighting any suggestion that there is anything wrong with themselves. They are likely to be suspicious of others, for they have learned that people are critical of them. They may redo their work two or three times to avoid errors, as they feel that people are more likely to tell them what they have done wrong than to praise them for what they have done well. Since they are more likely to expect attacks than assistance, they are defensive and will project feelings of hostility. In some cases this will result in their being attacked, and therefore, in their minds, they will have justification for their feelings.

Leaders who are low in flexibility have a considerable emotional investment in what they decide is right for them. Thus they will defend their position in what they decide is right with a great deal of intensity and energy. In their minds, they are being attacked, not their ideas. This inability to distinguish the difference may alert others not to argue with them but to avoid them. Consequently these leaders often misperceive their relationships with others. Often they tell us that one of their abilities is getting along well with others. They do not know that people are simply refusing to interact with them.

In some situations in which a company, division, or department is rundown and standards are loose or nonexistent, the addition of a leader with idealistic standards who refuses to compromise can have a dramatic turnaround effect on operational performance. The leader's fussiness about details, no-nonsense attitude, and fervor make it clear that he or she is in charge and that something is happening. Once the major changes have occurred, however, others will see the restraints and controls that brought them about as being too restrictive. In effect the low-flexibility leader has one set of standards regardless of the conditions. This is really at the heart of the meaning of flexibility.

In rare situations you may find a leader who has a combination of very low flexibility, very high introversion, and very high emotionality. This combination—if not recognized and dealt with—can, in stressful situations, become a pressure cooker in which the individual explodes in an outburst of anger. This scenario, when repeated, can be very disruptive in a work setting and result in considerable discontent and animosity among employees and colleagues who have been on the receiving end of such outbursts. Often, when supervisors confront leaders about this unacceptable behavior, they are contrite, sorry, and vow never to let it happen again, only to repeat the pattern time and time again. The definition of insanity is doing the same thing over and over and expecting a different outcome. Without real intervention these leaders will fall right back into their repetitive self-destructive traps.

Opportunism

Leaders with a high opportunism score see the world as a highly competitive, uncertain, and a risky place. Their motto is "Take care of yourself—no one else will do it for you." This attitude results in behavior that could be considered shrewd, manipulative, and socially expedient.

This attitude typically developed in childhood when security was missing to some degree and looking out for oneself had some survival value. Inconsistency existed in discipline, and the person was rewarded in subtle ways for what he or she could get away with. The individual learned how to bend the rules and push the limits. In people with above-average opportunism scores, we may find an early history of petty theft, truancy, or something similar. Out of this comes the philosophy that, simply stated, says, "It's all right as long as you don't get caught." Opportunism sometimes can be observed through "little white lies." It isn't necessarily evident at first blush, or during one's first interaction with the person, but over time it can become apparent.

As evidenced by some high-profile cases of executive white-collar crime, self-interest can cross the line from minor ethical issues to actual criminal activity. Leaders may create many opportunities for themselves that are legitimate, but some may exist in gray areas, where a less opportunistic person would consider them to be shady or unethical. Since self-interest stems from insecurity, as a person gains in wealth or position, the drive may lessen gradually. The individual is then able to defer his or her needs for broader considerations such as social status, recognized achievement, family, or statesmanship.

Leaders with a high opportunism score can be charming. They can say without compunction the things people like to hear said about them. A moderate degree of self-interest is usually an asset in social relations. It provides some "grease" or adroitness in social relationships where bluntness and absolute honesty might be disruptive. Leaders with a low score in opportunism are basically open and trusting. They may lack diplomacy or tact because they are direct and are not trying to do or say anything that would appear to further their own cause.

Introversion

Introversion measures individuals' openness and responsiveness to their environment. Leaders with a low introversion score are very open in their thoughts. Leaders who score high are likely to spend time in daydreaming, wishful thinking, or self-reflection. The reason leaders may score above average stems from their difficulty in dealing directly and openly with people. Self-conscious, bashful leaders who are unsure of themselves around people and who hide their feelings will score above average. Being this way, they tend to avoid directly confronting others or putting thoughts into action. Instead these thoughts and feelings become the fuel for daydreams. Essentially this is nonproductive behavior. Typically we like to see an average or below-average score for leaders on this measure. When high introversion is coupled with below-average initiative, we tend to see leaders who procrastinate. They think and think but never can make a decision.

Introversion is a characteristic that is helpful to understand, as it relates to other characteristics. We may think of the extrovert as the person who draws energy from being around others, whereas the introvert draws energy from being alone. That is part of what we are measuring. In addition it refers to how a person processes his or her thoughts.

Individuals who score low on the introversion scale tend to process things out loud and may or may not have much of a filter for what they say. Highly introverted people, on the other hand, choose their words carefully and wonder why the extrovert doesn't have more of a filter. There are pros and cons to both types of people. Assuming they are well integrated, both the extrovert and the introvert can be considered easy to work with, although they have different styles. If you're looking for people who are "quick on their feet," then individuals who score low on the introversion scale will meet your needs. If, on the other hand, you are willing to give people time to process their thoughts, there are no real downsides to hiring well-integrated introverted people. Usually highly introverted people are referred to as "reserved," because they do not share their feelings readily.

The introversion score is valuable in predicting peoples' leadership success as it relates to their level of emotionality. People who are highly emotional and score high on introversion hold in their emotions and stew about issues internally rather than deal with them in an open and direct manner. Time spent stewing about issues is nonproductive and unhealthy. People who are highly emotional but score low on introversion wear their emotions on their sleeves and may engage in little temper tantrums. Neither scenario is healthy or ideal, particularly for a leader.

Emotionality

The measure of emotionality consists of two major components that are closely related—manic behavior and depressive states. While we all are at times overly excited or enthusiastic, and failure causes most of us to feel somewhat depressed, people who experience either of these feelings to an above-average degree have difficulties. They tend not to be objective in their dealings with others; they also tend to overreact, take things personally, and become defensive. Productivity also tends to suffer with these types of leaders because they may be very productive when they are "up," but they become paralyzed when they are "down."

It is not at all that uncommon for leaders who are highly emotional to cover up their emotionality with a high degree of introversion. They have learned that society does not look fondly upon outbursts of anger or episodes of screaming; therefore they learn to hold their feelings inside. The group most negatively affected by a highly emotional, highly introverted leader is his or her subordinates. The subordinates don't know where their boss is coming from, because he or she is not open and tends to stew, which makes them feel uncomfortable. Without a doubt the best leaders are not highly emotional.

Satisfaction

Above-average scores on this measure indicate satisfaction or contentment. People with below-average scores say they are bothered by some situation or are generally frustrated.

This measure reveals how leaders see the world. If they perceive their experiences as beneficial and rewarding, they either had fewer "bad" things happen to them or have enough resiliency to accept what does happen. They may have a greater ability to recover when things go wrong, or they may have more or better ways of handling their environment.

People who score low in satisfaction express some pessimism or a feeling of futility or believe their efforts are ineffectual. These feelings could be the result of an unhappy childhood, an unfortunate marriage or other life situation, or a job that is not working out the way they had hoped. People who want success so badly they "can taste it," highly defensive people, or individuals who can't stop themselves from doing things they know are bad for them are also likely to score low in terms of satisfaction.

There is a difference between a temporary situation and long-term dissatisfaction. The variables of flexibility, opportunism, introversion, and emotionality can give clues as to the possible source of dissatisfaction. If a person has high scores in flexibility and low scores in opportunism, introversion, and emotionality, a low score most likely stems from a frustrating situation. On the other hand, if all of the other scores are unfavorable, the person's unhappiness or frustration most likely stems from his or her own character and behavior, not a situation.

In Summary

Although each of the individual characteristics tells a piece of the story, the combinations of these characteristics tell the whole story. As an example, we have found that leaders with low scores in initiative and persistence, when placed in leadership positions with a great deal of support, can function and their low scores may not be evident. But when these leaders are placed in leadership positions of stress or challenge without strong support around them, their low scores impede their ability to lead effectively and get things done.

When we compared individual leader assessment results to leaders' actual job performance, the perceptions of their employees, and our own observations, we found these personality characteristics and traits to predict leadership success. When we have given assessment results and coached incumbent leaders, we have seen them "self-develop" and enhance their own leadership abilities. Self-awareness, we have found, is a powerful agent of change.

A WORD OF CAUTION

Any leadership hiring decision is based on many factors. Although the WDI Leadership Assessment is very insightful, it cannot explain all there is to know about someone's personal psychology; background; technical competency; interpersonal, motivational, and communication skills, nor the level of energy he or she brings to the position. These and other factors must be ascertained through personal interviews, reference checks, and background investigations. The combination of these factors enables an organization to make the right hiring decision and ensure that the selected individual has the full potential and desire to learn, grow, and self-develop into an outstanding leader.

Chapter III

Work Value Analysis

We consider our research and work with work value analysis to be a pioneering application of the integrated psychological theory of leadership. We have found the management education and application of work value analysis to have a measurably positive effect on employee morale, job satisfaction, and trust in senior leadership. We have rigorously tested our employee satisfaction survey instrument to be "value-system free," ensuring that the survey results are not skewed or influenced by any one work value. We believe this is important when using an employee satisfaction survey to develop leaders in the use and application of work value analysis. As part of their self-development, leaders need bias-free, objective feedback from their employees.

Work value analysis is based on the original work of Dr. Clare W. Graves, professor emeritus of psychology, Union College, New York, and subsequent work by others who have studied and applied Dr. Graves's theory. Dr. Graves began his research on the levels of human existence in 1952 and continued his work until his death in 1986. He referred to his theory as "The Emergent, Cyclical, Double Helix Model of the Adult Human Bio psycho-social Systems." Graves's theory states, "The psychology of the nature of the mature human being is an unfolding, emergent, oscillating, spiraling process marked by progressive subordination of older, lower-level behavior systems to newer, higher-order systems as man's existential problems change."[8]

Graves's theory postulates that, starting from birth, a person progresses through consecutive levels of psychological existence. A person advances up the spiral of psychological existence based upon his or her changing life conditions and ability to gain and assimilate knowl-

---

[8] Graves, C. W. Fall 1970. "Levels of Existence: An Open System of Values." *Journal of Humanistic Psychology.*

edge. Change in a person's psychology usually correlates to changes in the conditions of his or her existence. Each successive level is a state through which the individual passes on his or her way to another higher level. At each level the individual has a unique psychology that is particular to that level of existence. At each level the person occupies, he or she adopts the value system and behaviors necessary to solve problems in life based on the psychology of that level.

The following diagram illustrates Graves's levels of psychological existence translated to work values.

Converting Levels of Psychological Existence to Work Values

LEVEL	EXISTENCE		WORK VALUE
7	Cognitive	➔	Freedom-Directed
6	Personalistic	➔	People-Directed
5	Materialistic	➔	Success-Directed
4	Saintly	➔	Structure-Directed
3	Egocentric	➔	Self-Directed
2	Tribalistic	➔	Task-Directed
1	Automatic	➔	*Doesn't exist in a workplace*

Inner- Versus Outer-Directed Levels of Psychological Existence

The process of moving from one level to the next is complex, but the movement does follow a pattern of either "outer-directed" or "inner-directed." The inner-directed pattern follows the path of levels 1, 3, 5, and 7. The outer-directed pattern follows the path of levels 2, 4, and 6. If a person is inner directed, the time spent on an outer-directed level will be short until he or she reaches an inner-directed level. The opposite is true for the outer-directed person. A smaller percentage of individuals are balanced between both the left and right brain, and one is not dominant over the other.

LEVEL	WORK VALUE	BRAIN DOMINANCE
7	Freedom-Directed	*Left-Brain Inner-Directed*
6	**People-Directed**	*Right-Brain Outer-Directed*
5	Success-Directed	*Left-Brain Inner-Directed*
4	**Structure-Directed**	*Right-Brain Outer-Directed*
3	Self-Directed	*Left-Brain Inner-Directed*
2	**Task-Directed**	*Right-Brain Outer-Directed*
1	Automatic	*Doesn't exist in a workplace*

Dr. Graves was truly a man before his time. A magazine article once referred to his theory as "the theory that explains everything." Today his theory has been validated by others and applied by those who have had the wisdom to recognize his great breakthroughs. Our management consulting firm has studied and attempted to apply Graves's theory since the mid-1970s.

Graves's theory of psychological existence opens up a whole new way to view and relate to employees. It provides a framework to identify job needs and formulate human resource management strategies, policies, and practices that can help companies achieve "best employer" status. There are others who have devoted their careers to refining and applying Graves's theory to the workplace. Among these are Dr. Vincent Flowers, Debra Heflich, and Dr. Charles Hughes. Their contributions to this field of study have aided our work significantly; in particular the assistance provided by Dr. Flowers and Debra Heflich in updating and enhancing our work value assessment has been invaluable. The reference section in this book lists these individuals and others who have made substantial contributions to this field of study.[9]

Industry Case Example

As leaders, when we devise human resource strategies, we should take into account the difference between employees who are inner directed (influenced from within themselves) and those who are outer directed (influenced by others). As an example we found that hospital registered nurses are 83 percent outer directed versus only 17 percent inner directed. You can imagine if RN recruitment and retention strategies were designed by an inner-directed leader for outer-directed staff RNs, the strategies would fail to meet the needs of the overwhelming majority of hospital RNs.

---

[9] Chronological Listing of Published Articles Regarding Grave's Theory and Applications. See "Work Value References" at end of this book.

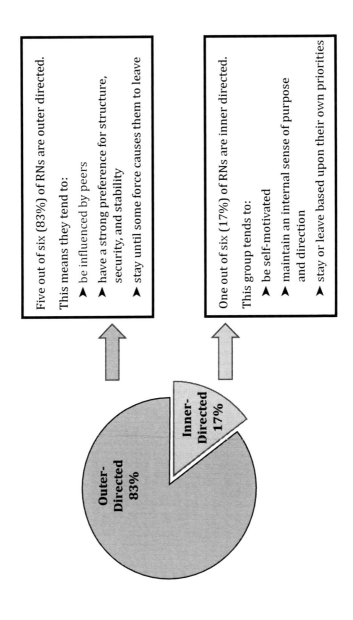

Five out of six (83%) of RNs are outer directed.

This means they tend to:

➤ be influenced by peers

➤ have a strong preference for structure, security, and stability

➤ stay until some force causes them to leave

One out of six (17%) of RNs are inner directed.

This group tends to:

➤ be self-motivated

➤ maintain an internal sense of purpose and direction

➤ stay or leave based upon their own priorities

Outer-Directed 83%

Inner-Directed 17%

Work Value Distributions

Work value distribution is the percentage of each work value found in any organization. It will vary by industry, by corporation, and by job category. Healthcare is a complex, labor-intensive industry. The hospital-wide distribution of work values presented below reflects the cultural, educational, and career diversification of that workforce. Because the nature of the work performed necessitates structure and precision, hospitals tend to employ a higher percentage of structure-value-system employees in staff and front-line supervisory jobs.

Work Value Distribution in Terms of Percentage of Hospital Employees

	Tribal Zone	Ego Zone	Structure Zone	Success Zone	People Zone	Existential Zone
Management	4	0	57	6	9	24
Physicians	4	2	55	9	9	21
Registered Nurses	5	0	67	5	11	12
Other Professionals	7	0	58	6	12	17
Licensed/Technical	10	1	66	5	9	9
Business Office/ Clerical	15	0	64	6	8	7
Skilled Maintenance	13	1	58	10	4	14
Service/Other Clerical	16	1	60	5	10	8
Security Officers	23	0	61	0	7	9
Average Hospital Distribution	10.8	0.6	60.7	5.8	8.8	13.4

Understanding Employee Work Values

Most of us are a combination of the above six work values, but one value is usually dominant. It would be unusual to see someone score 100 percent on one particular work value. There is no "right" or "wrong" work value; they are merely different. Below we provide a brief description of each work value. As you read these descriptions, please do not get hung up on the title or label. They are for easy reference only; there is much more to each work value than a simple label.

Task-Directed Work Value

These individuals have a strong need for safety and stability. They seek authority figures and are locked into traditions, rules, and rituals that they find difficult to violate. They are reactors, not initiators, and feel threatened by change. They derive their beliefs from their "tribe" (church, school, team, work group, etc.) or from an authority figure they respect.

The most important work preference for these individuals is a good leader. They prefer to work in a structured job that is routine and task oriented. For them the definition of a good boss is one who will tell them what to do and how to do it and who will work closely with them on a day-to-day basis. Job satisfaction comes from performing repetitive tasks in a rhythmic, routine manner and from receiving the boss's recognition for doing a good job. When it comes to communications, they prefer verbal communications between themselves and their bosses on a face-to-face basis. They prefer wages that are fair compared to those of other jobs similar to theirs in the community. The best merit-increase plan for these individuals is a fixed-step, in-grade system. They prefer basic benefit plans that provide protection and security, offered by a paternalistic employer who is looking out for them.

The Task-Directed Leader

Task-directed leaders work well in a group but do not like to work alone for very long. It is important that their superior give them feedback on their job performance as frequently as possible. The relationship with higher management is very important and is looked to for guidance and direction as to how the work must be done. These leaders work best in a well-organized job and will follow orders and do it the way their boss says.

Task-directed leaders relate to higher management that is personable and friendly but also firm enough to insist on getting the job done. If their boss is too distant or impersonal, they may react with a negative attitude and alienate employees from senior management. As much as possible, task-directed leaders should work in a group with others who share their beliefs. If they cannot be part of a group while supervising others, they need to be part of another group at meetings, breaks, and lunch. They prefer a boss who can protect them from arbitrary rules or senior management they perceive as manipulative. Feedback regarding their job performance should be ongoing and much more frequent than a once-a-year performance appraisal. Leadership behaviors these individuals should avoid include the following.

- Acting irresponsibly
- Not recognizing and acknowledging a subordinate's contributions
- Looking to subordinates for direction
- Becoming too impersonal
- Being overly compliant

Self-Directed Work Value

These are rugged individualists. They have moved out of the tribe and reject the belief that they need the safety and security of a "tribe" or the protection of a "chieftain." As far as they're concerned, they can take care of themselves. They are not concerned with what others may think and will quickly respond to any danger or threat to their own dominance or control. Depending on the degree of work value influence, they may find it difficult to psychologically live within the structured rules of society or the workplace. They tend to be persistent to the point of being stubborn. Because they want power, they respect it. Because they find it difficult to comply with the rules of an organization, these individuals tend to move from one job to another. The most important work preferences for these people are a job that pays well, does not tie them down, and has few, if any, rules. They only will respect a leader who is tougher than they are and who also will allow them to be tough. Pay is important as it enables them to buy things that make them feel important. Because they have no real loyalty to the organization, they eventually will leave if the job is not ideally designed to meet their needs. If a strong boss does not closely manage them, their non-adaptive behavior may manifest itself in continual conflicts with authority and may result in chronic absenteeism, sick-leave abuse, and tardiness. When it comes to pay, what-ever it is will not be enough. Job satisfaction comes from doing a tough job that is one of a kind and requires a great deal of ability.

The Self-Directed Leader

These leaders believe they are more creative and have better ideas about how to do the work than others. They are persistent, sometimes to the point of being stubborn about the things they think are important. They prefer to work alone rather than in a group, but they may like to be the center of attention and the unquestioned leader of the group. They tend to challenge senior leadership and can be disruptive. However, they will give respect to any boss who is more tough minded than they are. They tend to gravitate to higher risk jobs where they are recognized for their ability to handle adverse conditions.

Self-directed leaders need a boss who is experienced, older, and tough enough to control them, since they may have a hard time controlling themselves. Since they believe other people may be out to get them, it might just turn out that way, but they bring it on themselves. They typically are happier in smaller organizations where they can express their individuality with less constraint.

Leadership behaviors these individuals should avoid include the following.

- Failing to delegate authority

- Being too authoritative

- Becoming emotionally isolated from subordinates and/or senior leadership

- Requiring subordinates to compensate for poor or absent leadership

- Being too aloof

Structure-Directed Work Value

Conformist or structure-directed employees have moved from breaking rules to adhering to and enforcing rules. They are self-sacrificing and accept their role in life. They tend to be modest and self-disciplined. They are conformists with a strong work ethic and tend to be perfectionists in an imperfect world. They learned at an early age to be good and responsible and to do what is expected. They see this as their duty and expect others to do the same. They believe that it is good to make sacrifices in the present to obtain rewards in the future. They attempt to bring order into their lives by classifying people, ideas, and events into categories of "good" and "evil."

These individuals believe in predetermined fate and feel that forces beyond their control shape their destinies. They are oriented to duty, loyalty, and what they "should" do. They are motivated in life by the philosophy and values to which they have been exposed or with which they have been brought up, such as their religion or traditions. They prefer to see things in either black or white. They prefer work that provides long-term security and rewards their loyalty, hard work, and honesty. They work best in a clearly defined, well-organized job. They want job duties and performance standards that are in writing so that they know they are doing their job properly. They want to work for a structured, well run, benevolent organization. They like a consistent boss who can make good decisions. They do not like to work for a boss who has pets or shows favoritism. They prefer a compensation system that rewards longevity, loyalty, and length of service. Benefits are important because they provide long-term security for themselves and their family. They like to have human resource policies that are clearly written and explained in detail, including sick-leave, vacation, health insurance, and pension plans. They prefer benefit communication statements that emphasis the "benefit of the benefit." As a rule these employees tend to have the least absenteeism, tardiness, and sick-leave abuse.

The Structure-Directed Leader

Structure-directed leaders work hard at being good employees and supervisors. They generally complete their work on time, and it is thorough and within the specifications and rules. They do not care for bosses who are not as professional in their work as they strive to be, and they expect the same from their employees. They believe in long service and loyalty, and trust that senior leadership knows and appreciates their dedication. They can continue to work hard and long to get the job done, although they may get more hung up with the procedures than the objective. They make good leaders for task-directed and structure-directed employees and intuitively know how to handle self-directed employees. However, they may have trouble understanding and relating to individuals who possess other work values. Leadership behaviors these individuals should avoid include the following.

- Setting standards for employees that are too difficult to meet

- Projecting an image of superiority

- Being too much of a perfectionist and denying subordinates their approval because in their opinion the work is never quite adequate

- Delegating authority, with too many standards and rules that preclude subordinates from controlling their own work

- Being too rigid

Success-Directed Work Value

These individuals believe they can conquer the world if they can learn its secrets. Unlike structured-work-value employees, they are not controlled by authoritative beliefs. Rather they have a need to control or influence others. They believe that destiny is in their hands. They place a high value on achievement and measure their success by wealth and possessions. They are goal oriented, success focused, and entrepreneurial centered. As they thrive on competition, they may be active in gamesmanship and organizational politics. This sense of competition makes them feel they must win all encounters by defeating the opponent. They can be persuasive in their approach to others and may be disruptive in relationships if they push too hard in their attempts to persuade others. They view work as a game and money as the primary measure of success. Pay is extremely important, because to them it is "the name of the game." They prefer a job that is full of variety and allows them to wheel and deal. They prefer to be paid based on their results, so they respond favorably to variable merit-increase and/or bonus-incentive systems, if these systems are based on personal performance. They prefer a boss they think can help them achieve their career goals. They prefer to work in a job that offers opportunity for advancement and income enhancement.

The Success-Directed Leader

Success-directed leaders are highly competitive and goal driven. They are willing to pursue any strategy to win. If they are not careful, in their drive for personal achievement, they can paralyze subordinates through fear and intimidation. They can be creative and are generally good at coming up with new ideas they can sell. They work best where they have room to maneuver and where their personal ambitions are aligned with the company's goals.

Success-directed leaders use money as their way of keeping score. They are willing to bend the rules and stretch the intent of a policy to achieve work goals and get the job done. They prefer people like themselves as friends and tend to hire structure-directed employees as subordinates. Planning is an important aspect of their lives, and they will simulate plans under multiple scenarios. They strongly prefer to set their own goals rather than have someone else in the organization do it for them. They tend to be impatient with anyone they see as lacking drive, initiative, and ambition and who does not know how to play the game and get the job done.

These leaders seek jobs with upward career opportunities and keep on the move as they work their game plan. More often than not, these leaders tend not to provide enough structure, rules, and procedures for task-directed and structure-directed employees. Success-directed leaders must not let their quest for success alienate them from the employees they are empowered to lead. They need to spend time thinking about people as individuals, since they generally see them as numbers and resources to be used in achieving goals.

Individuals with other work values may not always understand the motives of success-directed leaders and may not trust their motivation or integrity. This is why it is important for success-directed leaders to communicate to employees in their individual work-value languages. When it comes to designing employee compensation plans, benefit plans, and human resource policies, it is strategically important that success-directed leaders recognize and accept that such policies and plans must be designed and written to meet the needs of employees with other work values and not just their own. Leadership behaviors these individuals should avoid include the following.

- Coming across as too manipulative

- Not being accessible

- Being too competitive

- Failing to delegate

- Paralyzing their subordinates through fear and intimidation

People-Directed Work Value

These individuals have evolved from self-achieving to helping others. They are people oriented and have a stronger concern for others than for themselves. They have a need to be accepted and place a high value on interpersonal relationships. They tend to be subjective and try to achieve harmony by understanding themselves and those around them. They are social in nature and have a need to belong. Belonging to and actively participating in a community are essential to their existence. They prefer social approval to individual recognition, cooperation over competition, and personal relationships over status or material things. They can become "rigid liberalists" and tend to champion liberal causes. The peer group to which they belong is important, for this is where they gain acceptance and from whom they derive their belief system.

They prefer to work in a job that provides a friendly atmosphere. They do not like conflict. They prefer a boss who "fits in" instead of taking over and who acts more like a friend than a boss. They want equality for everyone and management that treats everyone equally. They prefer group decision-making and consider the process as important as the product. To them the best committee is one that never ends. They prefer that management provide group recognition instead of individual recognition. They prefer open workspaces, communications in small groups, and 360 peer-review performance evaluations. Money is not a motivator, but if it is going to be used, they prefer it be on a team basis. They do not like merit pay that ranks one employee against the other. Motivation comes from peer-group pressure and humanitarian causes. They derive job satisfaction from helping others and developing interpersonal relationships.

The People-Directed Leader

People-directed leaders want admiration, caring, and acceptance from their subordinates. They can be rigid liberalists and come across as a bit opinionated in their views. They often have a difficult time delegating. They may tend to take on multiple tasks simultaneously without completely finishing any. They are more interested in getting along than getting ahead. Their feelings can be hurt since they are sensitive to others' feelings toward them. They really do care for people and try to relate well and easily to them, unless they see them as being exploitative. Interaction with fellow leaders and employees in groups and participation in committees is very satisfying. They resist working in an organization that they perceive as overly autocratic and impersonal in dealing with employees.

Since they put people before budgets, they may be less effective in financial management. People-directed leaders need to accept that others may not care for people in the same way they do and that they should not look to their subordinates to meet their personal socio-centric needs. Success-directed senior leadership may write these leaders off, as they view them as too process oriented and not results oriented. Effective people-directed leaders must provide more structure for their subordinates than they personally prefer.

Above all they must realize that others do not need and value personal relationships as strongly as they do, so they need to be tougher and more results oriented to be truly effective. Leadership behaviors these individuals should avoid include the following.

- Being overly process oriented versus results oriented

- Scheduling and spending too much time in meetings

- Engaging in unnecessary and long interpersonal discussions

- Being too subjective in setting goals and giving directions

- Avoiding making necessary decisions without a consensus

Freedom-Directed Work Value

These individuals occupy the "being" tier in Graves's theory of psychological existence. They tend to be unique existentialists who can rise above, understand, and relate to people at the other levels of existence in a meaningful way. They avoid conformity and tend to be creative, self-actualized, flexible, and adaptive. They also tend to be spontaneous, value common sense, and strive to keep life simple. They seek the meaning of life and will not attempt to convert others to their values or beliefs. For the most part, their psychological needs are met from within. They maintain an internal sense of direction and are guided by their own set of ethics and principles. They place a very high value on their freedom. They prefer an interesting job that offers freedom, autonomy, and the opportunity for personal growth. Money is important—not to buy material things but to ensure freedom. These individuals will accept any compensation system but avoid manipulation and generally are not motivated by incentive schemes. They are encouraged by opportunities for personal growth and development. They prefer a boss who works with them to set the goal then stays out of the way so they can achieve the goal in their own way. They prefer little—and do not require much—supervision and will self-report on the progress they are making toward achieving their goals. They are less interested in titles, job security, or status and more interested in job freedom, flexibility, and personal competency. They tend to be self-motivated and can tolerate ambiguity and rapid organizational change. They may tend to view company policies and procedures as bureaucratic roadblocks and attempt to circumvent them to achieve pragmatic results.

The Freedom-Directed Leader

Freedom-directed leaders typically do not require the same level of management as those with other work values, because their needs are met internally and do not need to be met by others. For them work, like life, is a journey. They are more interested in what they are doing than where they are headed. Money and promotions are acceptable but only if they enable these individuals to be in leadership positions that give them the freedom "to be." They will leave a job that is overly structured and restricts their freedom. They have a psychological need to be free, to learn, and to experience. They actually need nothing, although they will accept things and people. For example they do not need: security, for they will make it all right; power, since it is not necessary; structure, for their structure is in their mind; or people, since they can take them or leave them, depending on the situation. This makes them free to be.

The most difficult thing for freedom-directed leaders is to remember that not everyone sees the world as they do. They will have particular difficulty working for a structure-directed boss who does not understand their existential needs. Success-directed leaders may see them as a lazy version of themselves, and lacking ambition. Freedom-directed leaders need to provide much more structure to their subordinates than they think is necessary. If they are responsible for writing policies, procedures, or designing pay and benefit plans, they should seek input from structure-directed employees.

They must remember that 75 percent of employees have a different work value than theirs, and as leaders, they must adapt to their employees' work value needs. Leadership behaviors these individuals should avoid include the following.

- Being perceived as aloof or indifferent

- Not giving subordinates periodic feedback on performance

- Not being available when needed

- Not setting clear and precise individual and team goals

- Not being engaged in a meaningful interactive way

Case Study: When Work Values Clash

St. Elsewhere Health System consisted of four hospitals and approximately twenty clinics geographically distributed in a conservative city of four hundred thousand people. The health system employed approximately thirteen thousand employees, which included three thousand registered nurses and had a combined independent medical staff of approximately 1,200 physicians. The health system had an outstanding reputation for quality and was nationally recognized for its quality of nursing care. Its employee opinion survey scores increased for seven consecutive years, and it was regionally recognized as a "Best Place to Work." More than 50 percent of its managers and supervisors, 60 percent of its employees, and 68 percent of its registered nurses had a highly structure-directed work value.

At the top the system employed a CEO and a president/COO. The CEO had just retired and the board hired a national search firm to recruit—and advise them regarding—his replacement. A new external CEO was hired. He was charming, quick on his feet and had a very high success-directed work value.

Within less than a year, the new CEO had terminated almost all of the incumbent corporate vice presidents and replaced them with people who mirrored his own high success-directed work value. Within two years he had built a large, beautiful, state-of-the-art corporate headquarters to house the new VPs and the expanded corporate staff. In this facility the new corporate leadership team "brainstormed" to make what they considered to be "innovative" changes to the health system, which included changing its "corporate culture." Much of the change involved realignment of physician and medical services, external and internal marketing/public relations efforts, and considerable changes to administrative and human resource management policies and practices.

The new corporate VP of human resources mirrored the success-directed work value of the new CEO. She had a high level of energy and an acute sense of urgency to make as many "innovative" changes as possible within the shortest possible timeframe. She worked very hard to change the "corporate culture" to her and the CEO's vision. Within short order she implemented fundamental changes to HR policies and practices that affected employee compensation, benefits, performance evaluations, promotions, demotions, transfers, staffing, scheduling, and pulling. It was a wholesale change. Most of these changes were perceived as being purely economically driven. In reality none of the HR changes were "innovative." They merely reflected the new HR executive's prior experience in another industry.

On the medical staff front, physicians were hopeful the new CEO's promises of innovative solutions to the many challenges facing the healthcare industry would be realized. In the end these hopes and expectations were not realized. Instead decisions affecting centers of medical excellence, location of specialized physician services, and prioritization of financial resources were perceived to be self-serving to the corporation and not in the best interest of the physicians and their established medical practices.

As time went on, dissatisfaction with the new CEO and his senior leadership team's success-driven style of leadership grew into genuine lack of trust. The theme of distrust from physicians translated into what they perceived as manipulation and their not having enough meaningful input into decisions that affected their medical practice. The theme of distrust from employees and managers translated into what they perceived as too many wrong or unnecessary HR policy changes that created insecurity and devalued loyalty, longevity and length of service. This erosion of trust—combined with a general feeling that the CEO was "empire building" at the expense of the health system's other needs and priorities—created a nearly insurmountable chasm between physicians/employees and senior leadership.

After four years the board and the CEO, along with most of his senior leadership team, parted ways. The board replaced the CEO by bringing back their previously retired president and COO from the old regime. The medical staff and employees had a great deal of respect and trust for him. This was a high-level lesson regarding work value leadership. Today St. Elsewhere Health System is back to its old "successful" self.

Lessons Learned

The job of a health system CEO is a tough, demanding, and stress-filled position in a complex, sophisticated, and highly regulated industry with multiple stakeholders. The CEO in question here was a high-energy, visionary leader who in another organization may have done very well and stood the test of time. Unfortunately it just didn't work out at St. Elsewhere Health System.

I personally have worked with some truly great health system CEOs and I think each would appreciate the following advice to their governing board. Selecting the "right" CEO requires strategic thinking and a high level of due diligence; it can't be left to chance or to the sole advice of a search firm. The margin of error is too small, and the risk of selecting the wrong candidate is too great. A governing board should have in place a confidential CEO succession plan. If, at the time of need, an internal candidate is not available or not yet ready, they should proceed with hiring a highly ethical and reputable executive search firm to source and bring forth qualified candidates, but they also should retain an independent third party to interview and assess the candidates and conduct comprehensive background investigations that go far beyond traditional database searches or what a search firm normally would provide. This is why some senior members of our firm are retired FBI agents. A combination of the leadership assessment and comprehensive background investigation will go a long way to ensure the "right fit" and provide reasonable predictability of long-term success. I would give this same advice to a CEO who is selecting key senior-level executives such as a CFO, COO or CIO. This level of due diligence is beneficial not only for the board/CEO but also for the selected executive, as both can feel good in knowing the executive is the best person for the job and everything possible was done to ensure his or her leadership success with no second-guessing down the line.

In the case of St. Elsewhere Health System, the board didn't want to make another mistake so they brought their known, trusted, and highly respected president out of retirement to be CEO. This was a decision in retrospect they probably wish they had made in the first place, and maybe with independent advice they would have.

For any new executive, the following is work value advice to consider.

- Know and understand the work values of your employees because that is the "culture" of your organization.

- In the field of employee relations there are two truths—the truth as you believe it and the truth as your employees perceive it. Both are real, and decisions are made based on both. True communication only happens when perception is reality.

- Don't try to change employee work values; just accept them and work with them.

- Make all decisions that affect your employees based on their work value needs—not yours.

- Try to make your leadership style reflect the dominant work value of those you are leading.

- Don't hire direct reports who are mirrors of yourself, as you could spend a lot of time talking to yourself, about yourself, reinforcing your own misperceptions.

Case Study: Miracle on Main Street

Acme Medical Center is a one-hundred-year old, 350-bed teaching hospital located in a poorer area of a major city. It is a level-one trauma center where more than 60 percent of the patients are indigent. It is financially strapped and in dire need of major capital improvements. The working conditions are not ideal, and most of its employees are represented by a union, except for its registered nurses (RNs). The governing board recently hired a new system CEO in addition to its hospital administrator.

One day the hospital received a union petition for representation election notice from the National Labor Relations Board (NLRB) for all five hundred-plus of its RNs. The union filing the petition was a large national union that specializes in RNs. The union has a reputation for militancy and a track record of having won more than 90 percent of its union-representation elections. This same union represented approximately 1,800 RNs at a competing hospital within walking distance from Acme Medical Center, where RN wages, benefits, and working conditions were better. The union used some of these nurses to help organize and convince Acme Medical Center RNs to sign a union-authorization card. The union promised higher wages, better benefits, and improved working conditions. In its organizing literature, the union claimed that more than 90 percent of Acme Medical Center RNs had signed a union-authorization card.

The board and new system CEO called me in to assess the situation and offer strategic advice. The board member who called was an old friend and a highly respected healthcare labor lawyer. So, after a little thought, I saddled up and arrived two full days in advance of the board meeting to covertly gather intelligence and get a personal feel for the situation.

When I arrived I couldn't help notice the old run-down facility, worn-out furniture, high-volume emergency room, gang graffiti and activity, indigent patients waiting to be seen, and on the nightshift, some supplies walking out the back door. I had successfully consulted in hundreds of major union-organizing situations and knew from experience that this situation would take a miracle to win.

Fortunately, after speaking to several RNs from all three shifts, I found that miracle. You see, these weren't just any RNs; these nurses were special—very special. Every day they drove past another hospital where they could work for more money and better benefits, and in better working conditions, but they freely chose to work at Acme Medical Center because this wasn't just a job to them—it was a mission. Working at Acme Medical

Center was why they had gone into nursing. Here they were not just practicing nursing; they were treating the poor, the underserved, and the indigent—those who needed them most. Every day they went home tired and worn out but with great joy in their hearts, for that day they knew they had touched someone's soul and made someone's life better. These nurses were truly angels of mercy.

When I met with the governing board, I was equally impressed. They were sincere, dedicated community leaders who wanted more than anything to keep the hospital alive. They understood they were the front line of defense in the battle to save lives in this economically deprived urban area. I was most impressed with the board chairman. He was a classy, reserved gentleman who cared greatly for the hospital, its physicians, its employees, and most of all, its patients.

As fate would have it, to make matters worse, the hospital administrator resigned to take a job at a much larger hospital. In addition the chief nursing executive resigned as well. With the system CEO being relatively new, he could not carry the burden of a campaign alone. That left the chairman of the board to help lead what I felt was a necessary strategy to rapidly build trust and effectively communicate with precision in the psychological work value language of the nurses.

Under NLRB rules, once a union petition for representation election is filed, a hospital is under very strict laboratory conditions; it cannot make or promise any changes to hours, wages, benefits, or working conditions. In terms of communications, it cannot promise, interrogate, threaten, coerce, or spy. Employees have the right to vote for or against a union without such conduct or fear of retaliation. Because, under these rules, we could not conduct an employee opinion survey to identify issues and determine the RNs' work values, I used my experience to estimate their work value distribution. I estimated the work value distribution to be 50 percent structure directed, 30 percent people directed, and 20 percent task directed. It would be critical to communicate in both word and deed to these work values if we were going to have a chance at winning the upcoming election.

The union, with its team of professional organizers, had been organizing the RNs for months with numerous offsite meetings, media coverage, and cleverly crafted union literature. The hospital, on the other hand, had done virtually nothing, and now we had only a few short weeks to win the election. In the minds of both the union and those in the hospital industry, this was an impossible election for Acme Medical Center to win.

Our strategy was to rapidly build trust. To do this we needed to show that we not only understood the RNs' issues and concerns but also that we could relate to them. Only by doing this could we rebuild trust, and only then would the hearts and minds of the nurses be open to what we had to say. To accomplish this we had to rely on our abilities to properly diagnose, understand, and communicate both verbally and in writing the psychological work value language of the structure-, people-, and task-directed work values.

With the help and daily effort of a couple of other trusted consultants, we did three things. First, through the use of an anonymous question-and-answer hotline, we factually answered any and all questions the nurses had, which included what we knew were union set-up questions. Second, we worked closely with the nursing supervisors to educate and enable them to factually answer any and all questions their nurses had. Third, we arranged for the board chairman and CEO to meet with all RNs in a series of small voluntary group meetings to listen to and speak with them. Both the board chairman and CEO attended and conducted these meetings. They were sincere, honest, caring leaders who understood and spoke the work value language of the nurses and who cared deeply for them. There was nothing phony or contrived in these meetings—just open, sincere, and honest communication.

The first time the board chairman and CEO met with the nurses, they told them the union petition had caught them totally by surprise and that they were sorry it had to come to this. Then they just listened attentively; they let the nurses vent and tell them everything they thought they needed to know. These meetings were lengthy, difficult, and emotionally draining but very necessary.

The second time they met with the nurses, the board chairman told them with great candor and honesty about the hospital's dire financial position, the times they had to borrow money to meet payroll, and how much the board was trying to do everything possible to keep the hospital alive—not just for the patients but for them. He told them he knew it wasn't just a job for them but a calling, just as it was for him. In those meetings they laughed together, cried together, and bonded. You don't fool RNs; they are the soul of a hospital. The board chairman's heartfelt sincerity came through with every word, gesture, and facial expression. In all personal communication, 60 percent of what someone says is nonverbal.

The third meeting the board chairman and CEO had with the nurses took place two days before the election.

By then all of the nurses' union-related questions had been answered. This meeting was shorter in length. The board chairman and CEO told them they didn't think the union would or could do anything for the hospital. The union couldn't change their patient mix, give the hospital a needed cash infusion, or obtain more reimbursement for the hospital. They told the nurses they didn't think the union could do anything more to benefit their patients than what they themselves already were doing or what they could do by working together. Then the board chairman said, "I don't care how you vote, but I ask that you vote from your heart." He told the nurses he believed all decisions in life are based on one of two emotions—fear or love. He said, "Please don't make a decision based on fear; there is nothing to fear. When you walk into that voting booth, search your soul and vote from your heart, and know that no matter what happens or how the vote turns out we love you."

The vote count took place in the hospital auditorium. The room was packed with nurses, media, and onlookers.

The NLRB set up their tables at the front to count the ballots. Standing on one side of the auditorium were ten to twelve professional union organizers, and on the other side sat the board chairman, CEO, and a small number of other members from management. In the middle of the auditorium were rows of nurses.

As the vote count was ready to begin, I stood next to the head union organizer, a dapper gentleman from California. He had no idea who I was, and he didn't ask. Before the vote count began, I asked him, "How is this election going to turn out?" He said, "It's a slam dunk. More than ninety percent of the nurses signed cards and a petition that they were going to vote union." Well, the first twenty-five ballots that had been cast sure seemed that way, but as the count went on, it was apparent the union was losing. When the final ballot was counted, the nurses had voted nearly two to one against union representation. I turned to the man and asked, "What happened?" He said, "I have no idea." I asked, "Are you going to file objectionable conduct to the election and try to get a rerun?" He gave me a bewildered look and said, "Why?" Then he and all the other union organizers left the auditorium. After what seemed like an eternity, the auditorium broke out into cheers. Contrary to this union's usual practice, it did not file objectionable conduct to the election, and the NLRB certified the results.

Work Value Lessons Learned

For many reasons there is often distrust between employees and senior leadership. We measure this in our employee opinion surveys. We have found that if there is not trust, employee communication efforts fail. Trust is the conduit for influence; it's the medium through which our messages travel. If your employees don't trust you, your messages will be dead in the water. If they do trust you, their minds will be open, and they will listen to your messages. As a leader, to build trust you must be able to understand and relate to your employees; work value analysis enables you to do this.

When people communicate both verbally and in writing, they use nouns, verbs, and adjectives that reflect their dominant work value. If your dominant work value is the same as the person with whom you are communicating, you're in luck. But when you must communicate with employees in times of crisis—such as during a union election or another type of high-stakes scenario—there is no margin for error, and you can't rely on chance or luck. You need to know precisely: 1) what to say; 2) where to say it; 3) when to say it; and 4) how to say it. This sophisticated level of communication requires knowledge of work values, nonverbal communication, and neuro psychological emotional processing. When you're communicating to a person's work value with precision, you're not just talking; you're actually triggering within them emotions that are tied to their core belief system. Through the use of neuro psychological emotional processing (micro-facial expressions), you can see the emotional reaction on a person's face and know whether your message is getting through. Great leaders *are* great communicators.

To date the RNs at Acme Medical Center remain union free, but more important, with strong board and CEO leadership, the center is nationally recognized as a model for providing high-quality healthcare to the urban poor.

In Summary

Work value analysis is a valuable part of leadership development. When used with care and precision, work value analysis is a powerful and insightful tool for leadership self-awareness. It provides the missing link not only to understanding the psychology of those we are managing but also to understanding our own inner psychology and what we value in our jobs and how we think. What is always notable is the work value difference that exists between leaders and those they lead. This in itself is often an eye opener for leaders who receive this valuable insight for the first time. We commonly hear these leaders say, "I was flying blind" or "I got lucky. My employees' work values are the same as mine."

Of course we do not want to select leaders blindly, nor do we want to leave the success or failure of important leadership decisions up to chance if we can help it. Knowing the disparate work values of employees is essential to all leadership decisions that affect those employees. This information is also invaluable for leaders to know before they attempt to apply contingency, situational, or other types of leadership styles, as their style should reflect the predominant work value of the employees they are leading.

A WORD OF CAUTION

Work value analysis is a powerful and insightful tool, but it is not a means to know and understand all there is to know about human nature and employees' work-related needs. Work value analysis has nothing to do with personality characteristics such as dominance, self-confidence, independence, initiative, persistence, flexibility, opportunism, introversion, and emotionality. Rather work value analysis reflects how a person thinks and what he or she values and needs in work. Each work value has a range of functionality from positive to negative. There are no good or bad work values—they are merely different—and each has a place in the workforce. The secret to leadership is to know and understand your employees' predominant work values and then make management decisions targeted to those work value needs. This can be done organizationally as a whole and on an individual level by a manager.

Chapter IV

Leadership Assessment

The leadership assessment provided by Work Dynamics, Inc., measures personality characteristics and work values. In our experience this is a powerful combination that provides valuable insight into leadership selection, as well as valuable assistance in leadership self-development and decision-making.

When it comes to leadership selection, we want to ensure that candidates are void of characteristics that would make them difficult to work with and that they possess characteristics that enable them to make decisions and get things done. In our experience, regardless of how bright or how experienced a person may be, if he or she is difficult to work with or simply can't get things accomplished, he or she will not be successful. We have worked with many executives with impressive resumes.

However, when you talk to the people who work with them, they are not always regarded as great leaders, and sometimes they end up having to leave an organization under various pretexts because they were either too difficult to work with or the organization lost patience with them because of their procrastination and their not being able to accomplish much. In all our years of working with executives in multiple industries, it is our experience that the number-one predictor of great leadership is not a candidate's education or experience but his or her personality. The WDI personality assessment measures ten personality characteristics that, when viewed in combination, tell us whether a person is likely to be successful.

When you conduct reference checks on candidates, you typically get reasonably positive references. Does that mean when the person you hire is unsuccessful, the individual who provided the reference was untruthful? Not necessarily. Matching the right person with the right job, right boss, and right workplace culture is both an art and a science. It is important to note that a person who may lack the "ideal" leadership personality characteristics can be successful if the individual is placed in a supportive environment that offsets his or her weaknesses, but if and when that supportive environment changes, he or she suddenly may begin to flounder. If a person works in a highly supportive environment, some of his or her leadership personality failings may never be noticeable. However, if you put the person in a high-performance environment where he or she is under stress without support, those red flags suddenly can become problematic.

The WDI Assessment Process

The WDI assessment is available to client organizations. Clients are provided instructions regarding how to use the assessment for their leadership selection and development needs. Completing the assessment itself is easy, as it is web based, intuitive, and can be completed from anywhere at any time.

The Work Value Profile

The work value profile shown below provides the scores for each of the six work values we described. The work value scores are a distribution of points spread among the six work values, depending on how you answer the questions. The work value with the highest score is the predominant work value. The second-highest score is the secondary or backup work value. In the example below, "structured" is the dominant work value, and "people" is the backup work value.

CONFIDENTIAL

WDI Leadership Assessment

Date: 9-12-2012

Client: Any Corporation, Any Town, USA

Name: John Adams

Work Value	Score	Low		Average		High
		4	8	12	15	19
Freedom	12	**************************				
		8	12	15	18	22
People	16	***********************************				
		4	8	12	16	20
Success	6	*********				
		14	18	23	30	36
Structured	42	**				
		0	4	7	11	14
Self	0					
		6	10	13	17	22
Task	8	*******				
Percentile		10th	25th	50th	75th	90th

The Personality Characteristic Profile

The personality profile below shows a score for each personality characteristic we described. The scores range from 0–100.

CONFIDENTIAL

WDI Leadership Assessment

Date: 9-12-2012

Client: Any Corporation, Any Town, USA

Name: John Adams

Personality Characteristic	Score	Lowest	Low	Average	High	Highest
		10	25	50	75	90
Dominance	85	**				
Confidence	90	***				
Independence	65	******************************				
Initiative	80	**************************************				
Persistence	95	***				
Flexibility	60	***************************				
Opportunism	5	**				
Introversion	20	*********				
Emotionality	6	***				
Satisfaction	75	*********************************				

It is from these two graphic profiles that we provide our clients insight into both leadership selection and personalized leadership development.

A Word about Confidentiality

Each assessment is considered personal and confidential. The assessment report is provided to only one designated leader in the client organization who is accountable for leadership selection and development. Typically, depending on the size of the organization, this is the CEO, COO, or chief human resource or talent officer. Only those with an absolute need to know receive access to the assessment results. Once a candidate is hired or an incumbent promoted, the individual typically receives feedback regarding the assessment as part of his or her personal leadership development.

Case Studies

The following case studies provide some insight into how the leadership assessment is used to help select new leaders and assist existing leaders in modifying their leadership style and/or behavior so that they become more effective leaders.

Case Study: The Structured Leadership Candidate

ABC Corporation is a health insurance company with a division that processes health insurance claims. The company is in search of a senior vice president to run this division. The division employs approximately one thousand employees, with a mixture of professionals that includes physicians and nurses who function as utilization claim reviewers, along with information technology professionals and administrative support personnel. The division has struggled with budget overruns, information system problems, and slow claims processing.

The company felt the ideal candidate would possess considerable claims processing experience and would bring needed structure and management discipline to the job. An executive search firm was retained to conduct the search, and they presented three candidates.

All three candidates completed the leadership assessment. Below is the written leadership assessment of the candidate selected for the job, Ms. Jane Strong.

Leadership Assessment of Selected Candidate

Based on the work value and personality assessment profiles, we determined Jane to be an outer-directed leader. Jane is a structured, by-the-numbers, roll-up-the-shirtsleeves leader, who would place a high value on order, policies, and procedures. She would tend to be a stickler for the rules and doing things right and somewhat of a micro-manager in areas she thinks would require her personal attention. She would be detail oriented. She values loyalty and is a person of integrity. While she will demand hard work, loyalty, and conscientious effort from her staff, they will view her as a somewhat benevolent type of leader.

We determined that Jane has a strong personality, and her presence will be felt. She is comfortable in dealing with people and confident in her own decision-making. She is fairly independent and will not require a great deal of close supervision. She will plan her work and work her plan. Although she definitely has people skills, she will tend to have more of a functional versus participative leadership style. She has a very high degree of initiative and persistence, which means she is quite capable of gathering her own facts and making her own decisions. She will not require a lot of hand-holding and support from her boss when it comes to making decisions. Once she has made a decision, she has a strong amount of follow through. She is not one to waste a lot of time and has the capacity to stick with difficult work for long periods of time until the job is done.

Although Jane is somewhat of a perfectionist, she is not inflexible, but rather has a moderate degree of flexibility. She will not make changes for the sake of change, but she will adjust her methods and tactics and be open to new ideas if she is convinced there is a better way. She does not take criticism personally and because she has a low level of emotionality, she will not overreact in stressful situations, but rather will be cool, calm, and composed under fire.

Jane is a leader who will place the company first and herself second. She will make decisions that she believes are in the best interest of the company. She does not seek personal gain from situations and will not be self-serving. She values trust and will work to earn that trust. She is not one who will sulk or stew in her own juices; rather she is direct, open, and transparent. She is somewhat extroverted in nature and will have no difficulty meeting and relating to people. She is someone who commands respect and will give respect. Colleagues, superiors, and subordinates should enjoy working with her.

In summary we see Jane Strong as a well-integrated person with a strong personality profile and a structured work value suited for the situation. Although we would prefer her to be a more existential leader, given the challenges of the position and the need for more organizational structure, we see her as possessing the work value and personality characteristics necessary to be successful in the position.

Case Study: The Indecisive Leader

Midwest General is a five-hundred-bed tertiary hospital. Its chief operating officer of twenty-five years had retired, and after a national search, the CEO hired John Smith. John possessed impressive academic credentials and was well liked and respected in hospital circles but never had worked as a COO. Most of the department directors had been in their respective positions for quite a while. At the time of hire, the new COO had a number of initiatives he felt needed to be addressed, which included hiring a new CNO and achieving magnet status for the hospital. The CEO also had issues he needed addressed, including high RN staffing ratios and a subsequent higher-than-average compensation cost that was affecting the hospital's bottom line and subsequent bond rating. The expectation for change was high.

After one year on the job, the CEO became frustrated with the slow pace of change and lack of action. There were a lot of management meetings but little change. John was extremely well liked and got along with everyone, but he seemed to have a hard time making decisions in his own name. The CEO decided outside assistance was needed and asked Work Dynamics, Inc., to assess and assist John in his leadership role.

WDI Leadership Assessment

We determined that John's work value was balanced between people- and structure-directed. He is social in nature and has a need to be accepted by others. He prefers cooperation over conflict and is very process oriented. He places a high value on interpersonal relationships and prides himself on being a consensus builder. He is hardworking and loyal. He conducts himself in a professional manner and expects the same level of professionalism from his directors and managers. He genuinely cares for those around him and is kind and compassionate.

John's scores on personality dominance and self-confidence were strong. He will meet and interact easily with colleagues, physicians, and staff. He has a presence but is not overbearing or dominant. He is confident and self-assured.

John's low independence score combined with his high people-directed work value is impeding his ability to make tough, timely decisions, as he has difficulty being critical of people, or changing policies or procedures that his staff feels strongly about maintaining. Because John is more dependent than independent, he tends to appeal to those around him for support or direction. He may be doing this even when he has solutions in his own mind. In essence, John trusts the judgment of others more than his own.

John's initiative score was also low. Initiative implies the ability to establish priorities and make decisions independently, without the need to consult others. It is the taking of personal responsibility and making decisions in one's own name.

In contrast to John, leaders who score high on initiative do their own thinking and planning and have little need to consult with others before they act. The low-initiative-scoring leader such as John tends to seek and/or need approval or direction before he feels comfortable taking action. In essence, John works on the basis of team effort and what others think. Leaders like John, who have low initiative, tend to be indecisive and do not tolerate uncertainty or ambiguity well. They can get bogged down in the process of decision-making.

The combination of John's people-directed work value, low independence, and low initiative is overly influencing his desire to "lead" everyone to a "perfect decision" that they "accept." This need for "acceptance" is impeding John's ability to make tough, timely, and needed decisions. In essence John is having difficulty making decisions and taking responsibility in his own name. Because John does have a high persistence score, once a decision is made, he will have no problem following through and implementing the decision.

John has a high degree of flexibility. In their dealings with him, others view him not as rigid but flexible. He is a genuine person of integrity and sincerely wants what is best for the patients, his staff, and the hospital. He is not self-serving. If anything he may be somewhat naïve and trusting in his dealings with others. John's level of introversion is average, which means he is as open and responsive to his work environment and those who work with him as the next person. His level of emotionality is below average, which means he can handle stress reasonably well and will not overreact, but will be calm and collected when dealing with stressful situations.

Action Taken

Several follow-up coaching sessions were initiated with John to discuss the issue of slow decision-making. John subsequently came to the conclusion that because of his inability to make timely decisions, he was failing to demonstrate the required leadership characteristics of initiative. John admitted he had a fear of failure in his new position as COO. What became obvious to John was that his fear of failure was in fact causing him to fail because he was not achieving the goals he was hired to achieve. John did an about-face and began to increase his level of initiative and take more personal responsibility for decisions in his own name, even though some decisions were not acceptable to everyone. John has grown significantly as a COO and has turned his leadership weakness into a strength.

Chapter V

Desired Leadership Characteristics

Perhaps the first great leader to establish the importance of leadership characteristics was Sun Tzu in 400 BC. In *The Art of War*, he attempted to find common virtues in military leaders and settled on five: wisdom, sincerity, humanity, courage, and strictness[10]. He writes, "He who masters them wins; those who do not are defeated." Sun Tzu also identified five traits that are "dangerous in the character of a general." He listed these as: "reckless," "cowardly," "quick tempered," "delicate," and "compassionate." Sun Tzu believed each of these leads to defeat in some way.

We have found it to be a strategic advantage for a corporation to formally establish its own desired leadership behavioral characteristics that are expected from its leaders. By doing so it establishes desired

---

[10] Sun Tzu, *The Art of War*, ed. Samuel B. Griffith (New York: Oxford University Press, 1963.)

leadership behaviors by which all leaders can be judged, observed, coached, developed, and counseled. In many complex corporations, we have leaders who are technically the best in their profession but not necessarily great leaders. Having a clear set of leadership behavioral expectations from which to work makes it easier to coach, develop, and counsel these individuals on their behavior as leaders. It also places the responsibility for self-development squarely on the leader. We may be the best scientist or physician, but we may not be the best leader, at least not initially. Once the expectations are clear, we have seen some great technical specialists become great leaders. In our experience with coaching and counseling, we have found having a list of expected leadership behavioral characteristics to be invaluable.

The following are ten leadership characteristics we have defined and found to be most desirable in a leader. These desired leadership behavioral characteristics can and should be formally established by the CEO or adopted by the governing board. Whatever approach is used, these characteristics must be taken seriously and built into the annual leadership evaluation process if a company wants them to be effective.

- **Integrity:** Adheres to an uncompromising set of ethical and moral principles that are void of self-interest. Is direct, honest, and forthright in business dealings. Avoids "gray areas" or "shady deals."

- **Initiative:** Demonstrates the ability to independently set priorities and make decisions based on one's own thinking and planning, with little need to consult others. Takes responsibility and decides for himself or herself which facts are important and makes decisions on that basis.

- **Self-confidence:** Lacks self-consciousness in business or social situations. Possesses confidence and strength in one's own opinions, decisions, and abilities to address challenging circumstances.

- **Persistence:** Is able to stick with work for a long period of time without encouragement or prodding from others. Has the ability to persevere in the face of implied or actual resistance.

- **Flexibility:** Demonstrates the ability to adapt to changing situations. Under changing conditions, is able to compromise, adjust goals, or change tactics to achieve the desired goal.

- **Conceptual thinking:** Is able to identify problems and/or opportunities long before evidence of them is generally known. Thinks strategically and has a sense of vision.

- **Analytical thinking:** Has the ability to address complex situations and problems by breaking them into smaller pieces, organizing and comparing them systematically, and identifying causal relationships. Appears methodical and calculated in his or her approach to solving problems.

- **Motivational skills:** Is capable of rallying people to achieve a common goal. Has the ability to manage the emotions of others and focus their energy to achieve a difficult but desired outcome.

- **Communication skills:** Speaks with precision. Prefers straight talk and is adept at cutting through to the heart of the matter. Is an active listener, attentive to the other person's message, and provides verbal and nonverbal cues that signal his or her attentiveness and comprehension of what is being said. Is able to present and summarize a topic clearly and succinctly.

- **Interpersonal skills:** Has the ability to hear accurately and understand unspoken or partially expressed thoughts, feelings, and concerns and react appropriately. Is open, non-defensive, and easily gains rapport. Appears to have a "sixth sense."

We believe these desired leadership behaviors should be used as a screening tool in hiring leaders as well as evaluating existing leaders. We cannot measure all of these leadership characteristics through the leadership assessment process. Some factors—such as job-related experience, analytical skills, conceptual thinking, communication skills, motivational skills, and interpersonal relationship skills—should be assessed through personal interviews, reference checks, and background investigations.

If you adopt these desired leadership characteristics in your organization, you will select and develop effective leaders who will lead your organization to greatness. In any organization, when you have great leaders, the entire energy and dynamics of the organization change. People achieve more, give more, and expect more from themselves. It is *The Personality of Leadership* that builds great organizations.

May your life's work be filled with passion, and may you always lead with greatness.

Jim Velghe

For more information on WDI services and/ or speaking engagements, please contact Mr. Velghe at thill@workdynamicsinc.com.

Visit Work Dynamics, Inc., on the web at www.workdynamicsinc.com.

Work Value References

Graves, C. W. "Deterioration of Work Standards." September–October 1966. *Harvard Business Review.*

Flowers, V. S. and Hughes, C. L. March–April 1973. "Shaping Personnel Strategies to Disparate Value Systems." *Personnel.*

Flowers, V. S. and Hughes, C. L. July–August 1973. "Why Employees Stay." *Harvard Business Review.*

Myers, M. S. and Myers, S. S. Winter 1973. "Adapting to the New Work Ethic." *The Business Quarterly.*

Flowers, V. S. and Coda, B. A. January–February 1974. "A Human Resource Planning Model." *Personnel.*

Graves, C. W. April 1974. "Human Nature Prepares for a Momentous Leap." *The Futurist.*

Flowers, V. S. and Hughes, C. L. 1972. "New Goals in Personnel." *Management by Objectives.* Vol. 3. No. 4.

Myers, M. S. and Myers, S. S. 1974. "Toward Understanding the Changing Work Ethic." *California Management Review.*

Flowers, V. S. and Myers, M. S. May–June 1974. "Dollarizing Attitudes." *Atlantic Economic Review.*

Flowers, V. S. and Myers, M. S. Summer 1974. "A Framework for Developing Human Assets." *California Management Review.*

Flowers, V. S. et al. 1975. *Managerial Values for Working, A Nationwide A.M.A. Survey Report.*

Rohan, T. M. May 5, 1975. "Should a Worker's Personality Affect Your Managing?" *Industry Week*: 28–38.

"Multiple Communication Channels for Better Motivation." June 1975. *What's Ahead in Personnel*, No. 148.

Flowers, V. S. and Hughes, C. L. September 1975. "Toward Existentialism in Management." *The Conference Board Record.*

Flowers, V. S. *Values for Working* (videotape program). Dallas County Community College District.

Flowers, V. S. and Hughes, C. L. 1975. *Values for Marriage.* Dallas: Center for Values Research.

Flowers, V. S. and Hughes, C. L. January–February 1976. "Ego: Stumbling Block to Sales Success." *Marketing Times.*

Flowers, V. S. March 1977. "Who Do You Think You're Talking To? A Values Approach to Performance Reviews." *Supervisory Management.*

Flowers, V. S. and Hughes, C. L. January–February 1978. "Choosing A Leadership Style." *Personnel.*

Heflich, D. L. March 1981. "Matching People and Jobs: Value Systems and Employee Selection." *Personnel Administrator.*

Heflich, D. L. November 1985. "Those Who Lead, Follow: Employee Value Systems." *Administrative Radiology.*

Heflich, D. L. Fall 1990. "Value Systems and Employee Selection." *EMA Journal.*

Flowers, V. S. et al. 1991. *Value Systems Analysis: An Introduction.* Pottsboro, Texas: Value Systems Applications.

Heflich, D. L. et al. 1991. *Value Systems Analysis: Management Applications.* Pottsboro, Texas: Value Systems Applications.